Creamy Crème Brûlée Cookbook

Discover Delicious Crème Brûlée Recipes That You Can Whip Up at Home!

by Will C.

D1133721

Copyright Page

Table of Contents

Introduction

Want to impress people with a delicious and elegant French dessert? If so, this book is for you!

Filled with a variety of different recipes, this book has all kinds of delicious combinations that will satisfy almost any flavor profile. With simple ingredients and easy-to-follow instructions, even the most amateur baker can produce gorgeous-looking Crème Brûlée desserts! So what are you waiting for? Let's begin!

1) Classic Crème Brûlée

A classic Crème Brûlée recipe with a crispy, caramelized sugar topping

Makes: 4 servings

Prep: 30 mins

Cook: 25 mins

Ingredients:

- 2 cups heavy cream
- 5 egg yolks
- 1 tbsp. vanilla extract
- 11 tbsp. sugar

Directions:

Preheat oven to 325°F.

In a saucepan over med-high heat, add the cream by heating it until it's almost simmering.

In the meantime, whisk the yolks + 3 tbsp of the sugar in a large bowl until the yolks get a bit thick.

Slowly whisk the cream into the yolk mixture. Stir in the vanilla.

Pour mixture through a strainer into any container with a spout). Divide evenly among the four ramekins.

Set the ramekins in a roasting pan. Pour hot, boiling water in the pan so that it comes halfway up the ramekins. Bake for 20-25 mins.

Remove the pan from the oven. Let the ramekins cool for 1 hour. Then cover with plastic & refrigerate until cold, at least 2 hours, and up to overnight.

About 10 mins before serving the Crème brulée, pull the custards out of the refrigerator.

To caramelize them under your broiler, preheat it and set the top rack in the upper two-thirds of the oven.

Sprinkle the remaining 8 tbsp sugar evenly over the top of the custards, using about 2 tbsp per ramekin.

If using a butane torch, carefully turn the flame directly onto the sugar. Broil or torch until the sugar turns brown, approximately 3 mins. Remove.

Let cool for before serving.

2) Chocolate Crème Brûlée

A classic with a twist! Delicious and creamy Crème Brûlée with chocolate!

Makes: 4 servings

Prep: 30 mins

Cook: 25 mins

Ingredients:

- 2 cups heavy cream
- 5 egg yolks
- ½ cup bittersweet chocolate, chopped
- 1 tbsp. vanilla extract
- 11 tbsp. sugar

Directions:

Preheat oven to 325°F.

In a saucepan over med-high heat, add the cream by heating it until it's almost simmering.

In the meantime, whisk the yolks + 3 tbsp of the sugar in a large bowl until the yolks get a bit thick.

Once the cream is done, add in the chocolate.

Then slowly whisk cream and chocolate mixture into the yolk mixture. Stir in the vanilla.

Pour mixture through a strainer into any container with a spout). Divide evenly among the four ramekins.

Set the ramekins in a roasting pan. Pour hot, boiling water in the pan so that it comes halfway up the ramekins. Bake for 20-25 mins.

Remove the pan from the oven. Let the ramekins cool for 1 hour. Then cover with plastic & refrigerate until cold, at least 2 hours, and up to overnight.

About 10 mins before serving the Crème brulée, pull the custards out of the refrigerator.

To caramelize them under your broiler, preheat it and set the top rack in the upper two-thirds of the oven.

Sprinkle the remaining 8 tbsp sugar evenly over the top of the custards, using about 2 tbsp per ramekin.

If using a butane torch, carefully turn the flame directly onto the sugar. Broil or torch until the sugar turns brown, approximately 3 mins. Remove.

Let cool for before serving.

3) Strawberry Crème Brûlée

Crème Brûlée with bits of strawberry pieces

Makes: 4 servings

Prep: 30 mins

Cook: 25 mins

Ingredients:

- 2 cups heavy cream
- 5 egg yolks
- 1 cup small fresh strawberries, hulled and halved
- 1 tbsp. vanilla extract
- 11 tbsp. sugar

Directions:

Preheat oven to 325°F.

In a saucepan over med-high heat, add the cream by heating it until it's almost simmering.

In the meantime, whisk the yolks + 3 tbsp of the sugar in a large bowl until the yolks get a bit thick.

Slowly whisk the cream into the yolk mixture. Stir in the vanilla.

Pour mixture through a strainer into any container with a spout). Divide evenly among the four ramekins. Divide chopped strawberries between ramekins.

Set the ramekins in a roasting pan. Pour hot, boiling water in the pan so that it comes halfway up the ramekins. Bake for 20-25 mins.

Remove the pan from the oven. Let the ramekins cool for 1 hour. Then cover with plastic & refrigerate until cold, at least 2 hours, and up to overnight.

About 10 mins before serving the Crème brulée, pull the custards out of the refrigerator.

To caramelize them under your broiler, preheat it and set the top rack in the upper two-thirds of the oven.

Sprinkle the remaining 8 tbsp sugar evenly over the top of the custards, using about 2 tbsp per ramekin.

If using a butane torch, carefully turn the flame directly onto the sugar. Broil or torch until the sugar turns brown, approximately 3 mins. Remove.

Let cool for before serving.

4) Nutella Crème Brûlée

Kids will be sure to love this Nutella Crème Brûlée!

Makes: 4 servings

Prep: 30 mins

Cook: 25 mins

Ingredients:

- 2 cups heavy cream
- 5 egg yolks
- ½ cup Nutella
- 11 tbsp. sugar

Directions:

Preheat oven to 325°F.

In a saucepan over med-high heat, add the cream by heating it until it's almost simmering.

In the meantime, whisk the yolks + 3 tbsp of the sugar in a large bowl until the yolks get a bit thick.

When the cream is done, add in the Nutella.

Then slowly whisk the cream mixture into the yolk mixture.

Pour mixture through a strainer into any container with a spout). Divide evenly among the four ramekins.

Set the ramekins in a roasting pan. Pour hot, boiling water in the pan so that it comes halfway up the ramekins. Bake for 20-25 mins.

Remove the pan from the oven. Let the ramekins cool for 1 hour. Then cover with plastic & refrigerate until cold, at least 2 hours, and up to overnight.

About 10 mins before serving the Crème brulée, pull the custards out of the refrigerator.

To caramelize them under your broiler, preheat it and set the top rack in the upper two-thirds of the oven.

Sprinkle the remaining 8 tbsp sugar evenly over the top of the custards, using about 2 tbsp per ramekin.

If using a butane torch, carefully turn the flame directly onto the sugar. Broil or torch until the sugar turns brown, approximately 3 mins. Remove.

Let cool for before serving.

5) Orange Chocolate Crème Brûlée

A classic combination of flavors- this is perfect for lovers of chocolate and orange.

Makes: 4 servings

Prep: 30 mins

Cook: 25 mins

Ingredients:

- 2 cups heavy cream
- 5 egg yolks
- ½ cup bittersweet chocolate, chopped
- 1 tbsp. orange extract
- 11 tbsp. sugar

Directions:

Preheat oven to 325°F.

In a saucepan over med-high heat, add the cream by heating it until it's almost simmering.

In the meantime, whisk the yolks + 3 tbsp of the sugar in a large bowl until the yolks get a bit thick.

Add in the chocolate to the cream and then slowly whisk the mixture into the yolk mixture. Stir in the orange extract.

Pour mixture through a strainer into any container with a spout). Divide evenly among the four ramekins.

Set the ramekins in a roasting pan. Pour hot, boiling water in the pan, so it comes halfway up the ramekins. Bake for 20-25 mins.

Remove the pan from the oven. Let the ramekins cool for 1 hour. Then cover with plastic & refrigerate until cold, at least 2 hours, and up to overnight.

About 10 mins before serving the Crème brulée, pull the custards out of the refrigerator.

To caramelize them under your broiler, preheat it and set the top rack in the upper two-thirds of the oven.

Sprinkle the remaining 8 tbsp sugar evenly over the top of the custards, using about 2 tbsp per ramekin.

If using a butane torch, carefully turn the flame directly onto the sugar. Broil or torch until the sugar turns brown, approximately 3 mins. Remove.

Let cool for before serving.

6) Blueberry Crème Brûlée

Fresh blueberries are the star of this Crème Brûlée recipe.

Makes: 4 servings

Prep: 30 mins

Cook: 25 mins

Ingredients:

- 2 cups heavy cream
- 5 egg yolks
- 1 cup small fresh blueberries, hulled and halved
- 1 tbsp. vanilla extract
- 11 tbsp. sugar

Directions:

Preheat oven to 325°F.

In a saucepan over med-high heat, add the cream by heating it until it's almost simmering.

In the meantime, whisk the yolks + 3 tbsp of the sugar in a large bowl until the yolks get a bit thick.

Slowly whisk the cream into the yolk mixture. Stir in the vanilla.

Pour mixture through a strainer into any container with a spout). Divide evenly among the four ramekins. Divide the blueberries between ramekins.

Set the ramekins in a roasting pan. Pour hot, boiling water in the pan, so it comes halfway up the ramekins. Bake for 20-25 mins.

Remove the pan from the oven. Let the ramekins cool for 1 hour. Then cover with plastic & refrigerate until cold, at least 2 hours, and up to overnight.

About 10 mins before serving the Crème brulée, pull the custards out of the refrigerator.

To caramelize them under your broiler, preheat it and set the top rack in the upper two-thirds of the oven.

Sprinkle the remaining 8 tbsp sugar evenly over the top of the custards, using about 2 tbsp per ramekin.

If using a butane torch, carefully turn the flame directly onto the sugar. Broil or torch until the sugar turns brown, approximately 3 mins. Remove.

Let cool for before serving.

7) Coffee Crème Brûlée

Chocolate Crème Brûlée with a delicious hint of espresso

Makes: 4 servings

Prep: 30 mins

Cook: 25 mins

Ingredients:

- 2 cups heavy cream
- 5 egg yolks
- ½ cup bittersweet chocolate, chopped
- 1 tbsp. instant espresso powder
- 1 tbsp. vanilla extract
- 11 tbsp. sugar

Directions:

Preheat oven to 325°F.

In a saucepan over med-high heat, add the cream by heating it until it's almost simmering.

In the meantime, whisk the yolks + 3 tbsp of the sugar in a large bowl until the yolks get a bit thick.

Once the cream is done, add in the chocolate and coffee.

Then slowly whisk cream and chocolate mixture into the yolk mixture. Stir in the vanilla.

Pour mixture through a strainer into any container with a spout). Divide evenly among the four ramekins.

Set the ramekins in a roasting pan. Pour hot, boiling water in the pan, so it comes halfway up the ramekins. Bake for 20-25 mins.

Remove the pan from the oven. Let the ramekins cool for 1 hour. Then cover with plastic & refrigerate until cold, at least 2 hours, and up to overnight.

About 10 mins before serving the Crème brulée, pull the custards out of the refrigerator.

To caramelize them under your broiler, preheat it and set the top rack in the upper two-thirds of the oven.

Sprinkle the remaining 8 tbsp sugar evenly over the top of the custards, using about 2 tbsp per ramekin.

If using a butane torch, carefully turn the flame directly onto the sugar. Broil or torch until the sugar turns brown, approximately 3 mins. Remove.

Let cool for before serving.

8) Lemon Crème Brûlée

Classic Crème Brûlée recipe with fresh notes of lemon

Makes: 4 servings

Prep: 30 mins

Cook: 25 mins

Ingredients:

- 2 cups heavy cream
- 5 egg yolks
- 1 tbsp. vanilla extract
- Juice of 1 large lemon
- ½ tsp. lemon zest
- 11 tbsp. sugar

Directions:

Preheat oven to 325°F.

In a saucepan over med-high heat, add the cream by heating it until it's almost simmering.

In the meantime, whisk the yolks + 3 tbsp of the sugar in a large bowl until the yolks get a bit thick.

Slowly whisk the cream into the yolk mixture. Stir in the vanilla, juice of one lemon, and lemon zest.

Pour mixture through a strainer into any container with a spout). Divide evenly among the four ramekins.

Set the ramekins in a roasting pan. Pour hot, boiling water in the pan so that it comes halfway up the ramekins. Bake for 20-25 mins.

Remove the pan from the oven. Let the ramekins cool for 1 hour. Then cover with plastic & refrigerate until cold, at least 2 hours, and up to overnight.

About 10 mins before serving the Crème brulée, pull the custards out of the refrigerator.

To caramelize them under your broiler, preheat it and set the top rack in the upper two-thirds of the oven.

Sprinkle the remaining 8 tbsp sugar evenly over the top of the custards, using about 2 tbsp per ramekin.

If using a butane torch, carefully turn the flame directly onto the sugar. Broil or torch until the sugar turns brown, approximately 3 mins. Remove.

Let cool for before serving.

9) Lavender Crème Brûlée

Crème Brûlée recipe with floral lavender notes

Makes: 4 servings

Prep: 30 mins

Cook: 25 mins

Ingredients:

- 2 cups heavy cream
- 5 egg yolks
- 1 tbsp. vanilla extract
- ½ tbsp. culinary lavender
- 11 tbsp. sugar

Directions:

Preheat oven to 325°F.

In a saucepan over med-high heat, add the cream and lavender and heat it until it's almost simmering.

In the meantime, whisk the yolks + 3 tbsp of the sugar in a large bowl until the yolks get a bit thick.

Slowly whisk the cream into the yolk mixture. Stir in the vanilla.

Pour mixture through a strainer into any container with a spout). Divide evenly among the four ramekins.

Set the ramekins in a roasting pan. Pour hot, boiling water in the pan so that it comes halfway up the ramekins. Bake for 20-25 mins.

Remove the pan from the oven. Let the ramekins cool for 1 hour. Then cover with plastic & refrigerate until cold, at least 2 hours, and up to overnight.

About 10 mins before serving the Crème brulée, pull the custards out of the refrigerator.

To caramelize them under your broiler, preheat it and set the top rack in the upper two-thirds of the oven.

Sprinkle the remaining 8 tbsp sugar evenly over the top of the custards, using about 2 tbsp per ramekin.

If using a butane torch, carefully turn the flame directly onto the sugar. Broil or torch until the sugar turns brown, approximately 3 mins. Remove.

Let cool for before serving.

10) Snickerdoodle Crème Brûlée

Creamy Crème Brûlée dusted with cinnamon on top – perfect for the fall!

Makes: 4 servings

Prep: 30 mins

Cook: 25 mins

Ingredients:

- 2 cups heavy cream
- 5 egg yolks
- 1 tbsp. vanilla extract
- 1 cinnamon stick
- 3 tbsp. sugar

For topping:

- 8 tbsp. sugar
- 4 tsp. cinnamon

Directions:

Preheat oven to 325°F.

In a saucepan over med-high heat, add the cream by heating it until it's almost simmering. Add in the cinnamon stick.

In the meantime, whisk the yolks + 3 tbsp of the sugar in a large bowl until the yolks get a bit thick.

Once the cream is done, remove the stick.

Slowly whisk the cream into the yolk mixture. Stir in the vanilla.

Pour mixture through a strainer into any container with a spout). Divide evenly among the four ramekins.

Set the ramekins in a roasting pan. Pour hot, boiling water in the pan so that it comes halfway up the ramekins. Bake for 20-25 mins.

Remove the pan from the oven. Let the ramekins cool for 1 hour. Then cover with plastic & refrigerate until cold, at least 2 hours, and up to overnight.

About 10 mins before serving the Crème brulée, pull the custards out of the refrigerator.

To caramelize them under your broiler, preheat it and set the top rack in the upper two-thirds of the oven.

Sprinkle the remaining 8 tbsp sugar and 4 tsp cinnamon evenly over the top of the custards.

If using a butane torch, carefully turn the flame directly onto the sugar. Broil or torch until the sugar turns brown, approximately 3 mins. Remove.

Let cool for before serving.

11) Coconut Crème Brûlée

A delicious and easy coconut-flavored Crème Brûlée recipe!

Makes: 4 servings

Prep: 30 mins

Cook: 25 mins

Ingredients:

- 2 cups coconut milk
- 5 egg yolks
- 1 tbsp. vanilla extract
- 11 tbsp. sugar

Directions:

Preheat oven to 325°F.

In a saucepan over med-high heat, add the coconut milk by heating it until it's almost simmering.

In the meantime, whisk the yolks + 3 tbsp of the sugar in a large bowl until the yolks get a bit thick.

Slowly whisk coconut milk into the yolk mixture. Stir in the vanilla.

Pour mixture through a strainer into any container with a spout). Divide evenly among the four ramekins.

Set the ramekins in a roasting pan. Pour hot, boiling water in the pan so that it comes halfway up the ramekins. Bake for 20-25 mins.

Remove the pan from the oven. Let the ramekins cool for 1 hour. Then cover with plastic & refrigerate until cold, at least 2 hours, and up to overnight.

About 10 mins before serving the Crème brulée, pull the custards out of the refrigerator.

To caramelize them under your broiler, preheat it and set the top rack in the upper two-thirds of the oven.

Sprinkle the remaining 8 tbsp sugar evenly over the top of the custards, using about 2 tbsp per ramekin.

If using a butane torch, carefully turn the flame directly onto the sugar. Broil or torch until the sugar turns brown, approximately 3 mins. Remove.

Let cool for before serving.

12) Raspberry Crème Brûlée

Delicious Crème Brûlée with raspberries – perfect for the summer months!

Makes: 4 servings

Prep: 30 mins

Cook: 25 mins

Ingredients:

- 2 cups heavy cream
- 5 egg yolks
- 1 cup small fresh raspberries, halved
- 1 tbsp. vanilla extract
- 11 tbsp. sugar

Directions:

Preheat oven to 325°F.

In a saucepan over med-high heat, add the cream by heating it until it's almost simmering.

In the meantime, whisk the yolks + 3 tbsp of the sugar in a large bowl until the yolks get a bit thick.

Slowly whisk the cream into the yolk mixture. Stir in the vanilla.

Pour mixture through a strainer into any container with a spout). Divide evenly among the four ramekins. Divide the raspberries between ramekins.

Set the ramekins in a roasting pan. Pour hot, boiling water in the pan so that it comes halfway up the ramekins. Bake for 20-25 mins.

Remove the pan from the oven. Let the ramekins cool for 1 hour. Then cover with plastic & refrigerate until cold, at least 2 hours, and up to overnight.

About 10 mins before serving the Crème brulée, pull the custards out of the refrigerator.

To caramelize them under your broiler, preheat it and set the top rack in the upper two-thirds of the oven.

Sprinkle the remaining 8 tbsp sugar evenly over the top of the custards, using about 2 tbsp per ramekin.

If using a butane torch, carefully turn the flame directly onto the sugar. Broil or torch until the sugar turns brown, approximately 3 mins. Remove.

Let cool for before serving.

13) White Chocolate Coffee Crème Brûlée

Sweet white chocolate Crème Brûlée with a touch of bitter coffee

Makes: 4 servings

Prep: 30 mins

Cook: 25 mins

Ingredients:

- 2 cups heavy cream
- 5 egg yolks
- 1 tbsp. vanilla extract
- ½ cup white chocolate, chopped
- 1 tbsp. coffee
- 11 tbsp. sugar

Directions:

Preheat oven to 325°F.

In a saucepan over med-high heat, add the cream by heating it until it's almost simmering.

In the meantime, whisk the yolks + 3 tbsp of the sugar in a large bowl until the yolks get a bit thick.

Once the cream is done, add in the chocolate and coffee.

Then slowly whisk cream and chocolate mixture into the yolk mixture. Stir in the vanilla.

Pour mixture through a strainer into any container with a spout). Divide evenly among the four ramekins.

Set the ramekins in a roasting pan. Pour hot, boiling water in the pan so that it comes halfway up the ramekins. Bake for 20-25 mins.

Remove the pan from the oven. Let the ramekins cool for 1 hour. Then cover with plastic & refrigerate until cold, at least 2 hours, and up to overnight.

About 10 mins before serving the Crème brulée, pull the custards out of the refrigerator.

To caramelize them under your broiler, preheat it and set the top rack in the upper two-thirds of the oven.

Sprinkle the remaining 8 tbsp sugar evenly over the top of the custards, using about 2 tbsp per ramekin.

If using a butane torch, carefully turn the flame directly onto the sugar. Broil or torch until the sugar turns brown, approximately 3 mins. Remove.

Let cool for before serving.

14) Key Lime Crème Brûlée

A delicious key lime pie Crème Brûlée recipe with fresh notes of lime.

Makes: 4 servings

Prep: 30 mins

Cook: 25 mins

Ingredients:

- 2 cups heavy cream
- 5 egg yolks
- 1 tbsp. vanilla extract
- Juice of 1 large lime
- ½ tsp. lemon zest
- 11 tbsp. sugar

Directions:

Preheat oven to 325°F.

In a saucepan over a med-high heat, add the cream by heating it until it's almost simmering.

In the meantime, whisk the yolks + 3 tbsp of the sugar in a large bowl until the yolks get a bit thick.

Slowly whisk cream into the yolk mixture. Stir in the vanilla, juice and zest.

Pour mixture through a strainer into any container with a spout). Divide evenly among the four ramekins.

Set the ramekins in a roasting pan. Pour hot, boiling water in the pan so that is comes half up the ramekins. Bake for 20-25 mins.

Remove pan from the oven. Let the ramekins cool for 1 hour. Then cover with plastic & refrigerate until cold, at least 2 hours and up to overnight.

About 10 mins before serving the Crème brulée, pull the custards out of the refrigerator.

To caramelize them under your broiler, preheat it and set the top rack in the upper two-thirds of the oven.

Sprinkle the remaining 8 tbsp sugar evenly over the top of the custards, using about 2 tbsp per ramekin.

If using a butane torch, carefully turn the flame directly onto the sugar. Broil or torch until the sugar turns brown, approximately 3 mins. Remove.

Let cool for before serving.

15) Green Tea Crème Brûlée

Matcha lovers rejoice! This creamy matcha Crème Brûlée is a perfect bittersweet dessert.

Makes: 4 servings

Prep: 30 mins

Cook: 25 mins

Ingredients:

- 2 cups heavy cream
- 5 egg yolks
- 1 tbsp. vanilla extract
- 1 tbsp. matcha
- 11 tbsp. sugar

Directions:

Preheat oven to 325°F.

In a saucepan over med-high heat, add the cream by heating it until it's almost simmering.

In the meantime, whisk the yolks + 3 tbsp of the sugar in a large bowl until the yolks get a bit thick.

Slowly whisk the cream into the yolk mixture. Stir in the vanilla and matcha.

Pour mixture through a strainer into any container with a spout). Divide evenly among the four ramekins.

Set the ramekins in a roasting pan. Pour hot, boiling water in the pan so that it comes halfway up the ramekins. Bake for 20-25 mins.

Remove the pan from the oven. Let the ramekins cool for 1 hour. Then cover with plastic & refrigerate until cold, at least 2 hours, and up to overnight.

About 10 mins before serving the Crème brulée, pull the custards out of the refrigerator.

To caramelize them under your broiler, preheat it and set the top rack in the upper two-thirds of the oven.

Sprinkle the remaining 8 tbsp sugar evenly over the top of the custards, using about 2 tbsp per ramekin.

If using a butane torch, carefully turn the flame directly onto the sugar. Broil or torch until the sugar turns brown, approximately 3 mins. Remove.

Let cool for before serving.

16) Peach Crème Brûlée

Creamy vanilla Crème Brûlée with pieces of fresh peaches on top

Makes: 4 servings

Prep: 30 mins

Cook: 25 mins

Ingredients:

- 2 cups heavy cream
- 5 egg yolks
- 1 tbsp. vanilla extract
- 1 ripe peach, cut into cubes
- 11 tbsp. sugar

Directions:

Preheat oven to 325°F.

In a saucepan over med-high heat, add the cream by heating it until it's almost simmering.

In the meantime, whisk the yolks + 3 tbsp of the sugar in a large bowl until the yolks get a bit thick.

Then slowly whisk the cream into the yolk mixture. Stir in the vanilla.

Pour mixture through a strainer into any container with a spout). Divide evenly among the four ramekins and top with peaches.

Set the ramekins in a roasting pan. Pour hot, boiling water in the pan so that it comes halfway up the ramekins. Bake for 20-25 mins.

Remove the pan from the oven. Let the ramekins cool for 1 hour. Then cover with plastic & refrigerate until cold, at least 2 hours, and up to overnight.

About 10 mins before serving the Crème brulée, pull the custards out of the refrigerator.

To caramelize them under your broiler, preheat it and set the top rack in the upper two-thirds of the oven.

Sprinkle the remaining 8 tbsp sugar evenly over the top of the custards, using about 2 tbsp per ramekin.

If using a butane torch, carefully turn the flame directly onto the sugar. Broil or torch until the sugar turns brown, approximately 3 mins. Remove.

Let cool for before serving.

17) Dark Chocolate Crème Brûlée

Lovers of dark chocolate are sure to love this recipe!

Makes: 4 servings

Prep: 30 mins

Cook: 25 mins

Ingredients:

- 2 cups heavy cream
- 5 egg yolks
- ½ cup dark chocolate, chopped
- 1 tbsp. vanilla extract
- 11 tbsp. sugar

Directions:

Preheat oven to 325°F.

In a saucepan over med-high heat, add the cream by heating it until it's almost simmering.

In the meantime, whisk the yolks + 3 tbsp of the sugar in a large bowl until the yolks get a bit thick.

Once the cream is done, add in the chocolate.

Then slowly whisk cream and chocolate mixture into the yolk mixture. Stir in the vanilla.

Pour mixture through a strainer into any container with a spout). Divide evenly among the four ramekins.

Set the ramekins in a roasting pan. Pour hot, boiling water in the pan so that it comes halfway up the ramekins. Bake for 20-25 mins.

Remove the pan from the oven. Let the ramekins cool for 1 hour. Then cover with plastic & refrigerate until cold, at least 2 hours, and up to overnight.

About 10 mins before serving the Crème brulée, pull the custards out of the refrigerator.

To caramelize them under your broiler, preheat it and set the top rack in the upper two-thirds of the oven.

Sprinkle the remaining 8 tbsp sugar evenly over the top of the custards, using about 2 tbsp per ramekin.

If using a butane torch, carefully turn the flame directly onto the sugar. Broil or torch until the sugar turns brown, approximately 3 mins. Remove.

Let cool for before serving.

18) Maple Syrup Crème Brûlée

Crème Brûlée recipe with sweet maple syrup – a good option for brunch!

Makes: 4 servings

Prep: 30 mins

Cook: 25 mins

Ingredients:

- 2 cups heavy cream
- 5 egg yolks
- 1 tbsp. vanilla extract
- 11 tbsp. sugar
- 1 tbsp. maple syrup

Directions:

Preheat oven to 325°F.

In a saucepan over med-high heat, add the cream by heating it until it's almost simmering.

In the meantime, whisk the yolks + 3 tbsp of the sugar in a large bowl until the yolks get a bit thick.

Slowly whisk the cream into the yolk mixture. Stir in the vanilla and maple syrup.

Pour mixture through a strainer into any container with a spout). Divide evenly among the four ramekins.

Set the ramekins in a roasting pan. Pour hot, boiling water in the pan so that it comes halfway up the ramekins. Bake for 20-25 mins.

Remove the pan from the oven. Let the ramekins cool for 1 hour. Then cover with plastic & refrigerate until cold, at least 2 hours, and up to overnight.

About 10 mins before serving the Crème brulée, pull the custards out of the refrigerator.

To caramelize them under your broiler, preheat it and set the top rack in the upper two-thirds of the oven.

Sprinkle the remaining 8 tbsp sugar evenly over the top of the custards, using about 2 tbsp per ramekin.

If using a butane torch, carefully turn the flame directly onto the sugar. Broil or torch until the sugar turns brown, approximately 3 mins. Remove.

Let cool for before serving.

19) Pistachio Crème Brûlée

Crème Brûlée with crushed pistachios.

Makes: 4 servings

Prep: 30 mins

Cook: 25 mins

Ingredients:

- 2 cups heavy cream
- 5 egg yolks
- 1 tbsp. vanilla extract
- 11 tbsp. sugar
- 2 tbsp. crushed pistachios, plus extra for topping

Directions:

Preheat oven to 325°F.

In a saucepan over med-high heat, add the cream by heating it until it's almost simmering.

In the meantime, whisk the yolks + 3 tbsp of the sugar in a large bowl until the yolks get a bit thick.

Slowly whisk the cream into the yolk mixture. Stir in the vanilla and pistachios.

Pour mixture through a strainer into any container with a spout). Divide evenly among the four ramekins.

Set the ramekins in a roasting pan. Pour hot, boiling water in the pan so that it comes halfway up the ramekins. Bake for 20-25 mins.

Remove the pan from the oven. Let the ramekins cool for 1 hour. Then cover with plastic & refrigerate until cold, at least 2 hours, and up to overnight.

About 10 mins before serving the Crème brulée, pull the custards out of the refrigerator.

To caramelize them under your broiler, preheat it and set the top rack in the upper two-thirds of the oven.

Sprinkle the remaining 8 tbsp sugar evenly over the top of the custards, using about 2 tbsp per ramekin.

If using a butane torch, carefully turn the flame directly onto the sugar. Broil or torch until the sugar turns brown, approximately 3 mins. Remove.

Let cool for before serving. Serve with additional pistachios on top.

20) Cinnamon Honey Crème Brûlée

This recipe is perfect for the colder months – sweet honey and toasty cinnamon flavors!

Makes: 4 servings

Prep: 30 mins

Cook: 25 mins

Ingredients:

- 2 cups heavy cream
- 5 egg yolks
- 1 tbsp. vanilla extract
- 8 tbsp. sugar
- 3 tbsp. honey
- 1 tsp. cinnamon

Directions:

Preheat oven to 325°F.

In a saucepan over med-high heat, add the cream by heating it until it's almost simmering.

In the meantime, whisk the yolks + 3 tbsp of the sugar in a large bowl until the yolks get a bit thick. Add in the honey next.

Slowly whisk the cream into the yolk mixture. Stir in the vanilla and cinnamon.

Pour mixture through a strainer into any container with a spout). Divide evenly among the four ramekins.

Set the ramekins in a roasting pan. Pour hot, boiling water in the pan so that it comes halfway up the ramekins. Bake for 20-25 mins.

Remove the pan from the oven. Let the ramekins cool for 1 hour. Then cover with plastic & refrigerate until cold, at least 2 hours, and up to overnight.

About 10 mins before serving the Crème brulée, pull the custards out of the refrigerator.

To caramelize them under your broiler, preheat it and set the top rack in the upper two-thirds of the oven.

Sprinkle the remaining 8 tbsp sugar evenly over the top of the custards, using about 2 tbsp per ramekin.

If using a butane torch, carefully turn the flame directly onto the sugar. Broil or torch until the sugar turns brown, approximately 3 mins. Remove.

Let cool for before serving.

21) Apple Crème Brûlée

Creamy apple Crème Brûlée with cinnamon.

Makes: 4 servings

Prep: 30 mins

Cook: 25 mins

Ingredients:

- 2 cups heavy cream
- 5 egg yolks
- 1 cup apple, peeled and diced
- 1 tbsp. vanilla extract
- 11 tbsp. sugar
- 1 tsp. cinnamon

Directions:

Preheat oven to 325°F.

In a saucepan over med-high heat, add the cream by heating it until it's almost simmering.

In the meantime, whisk the yolks + 3 tbsp of the sugar in a large bowl until the yolks get a bit thick.

Slowly whisk the cream into the yolk mixture. Stir in the vanilla and cinnamon.

Pour mixture through a strainer into any container with a spout). Divide evenly among the four ramekins. Divide the apples among the ramekins too.

Set the ramekins in a roasting pan. Pour hot, boiling water in the pan so that it comes halfway up the ramekins. Bake for 20-25 mins.

Remove the pan from the oven. Let the ramekins cool for 1 hour. Then cover with plastic & refrigerate until cold, at least 2 hours, and up to overnight.

About 10 mins before serving the Crème brulée, pull the custards out of the refrigerator.

To caramelize them under your broiler, preheat it and set the top rack in the upper two-thirds of the oven.

Sprinkle the remaining 8 tbsp sugar evenly over the top of the custards, using about 2 tbsp per ramekin.

If using a butane torch, carefully turn the flame directly onto the sugar. Broil or torch until the sugar turns brown, approximately 3 mins. Remove.

Let cool for before serving.

22) Biscoff Crème Brûlée

Delicious biscoff Crème Brûlée that kids will absolutely love!

Makes: 4 servings

Prep: 30 mins

Cook: 25 mins

Ingredients:

- 2 cups heavy cream
- 5 egg yolks
- ½ cup Biscoff spread
- 11 tbsp. sugar

Directions:

Preheat oven to 325°F.

In a saucepan over med-high heat, add the cream by heating it until it's almost simmering.

In the meantime, whisk the yolks + 3 tbsp of the sugar in a large bowl until the yolks get a bit thick.

When the cream is done, add in the Biscoff.

Then slowly whisk the cream mixture into the yolk mixture.

Pour mixture through a strainer into any container with a spout). Divide evenly among the four ramekins.

Set the ramekins in a roasting pan. Pour hot, boiling water in the pan so that it comes halfway up the ramekins. Bake for 20-25 mins.

Remove the pan from the oven. Let the ramekins cool for 1 hour. Then cover with plastic & refrigerate until cold, at least 2 hours, and up to overnight.

About 10 mins before serving the Crème brulée, pull the custards out of the refrigerator.

To caramelize them under your broiler, preheat it and set the top rack in the upper two-thirds of the oven.

Sprinkle the remaining 8 tbsp sugar evenly over the top of the custards, using about 2 tbsp per ramekin.

If using a butane torch, carefully turn the flame directly onto the sugar. Broil or torch until the sugar turns brown, approximately 3 mins. Remove.

Let cool for before serving.

23) Oreo Crème Brûlée

Crème Brûlée with pieces of Oreo and Oreo filling

Makes: 4 servings

Prep: 30 mins

Cook: 25 mins

Ingredients:

- 2 cups heavy cream
- 5 egg yolks
- 8 Oreo cookies
- 1 tbsp. vanilla extract
- 11 tbsp. sugar

Directions:

Preheat oven to 325°F.

Separate the Oreo filling and the cookies. Place filling in one bowl and cookies in another. Crush the cookies and keep them aside.

In a saucepan over med-high heat, add the cream by heating it until it's almost simmering. Add in the filling.

In the meantime, whisk the yolks + 3 tbsp of the sugar in a large bowl until the yolks get a bit thick.

Then slowly whisk the cream mixture into the yolk mixture. Stir in the vanilla

Pour mixture through a strainer into any container with a spout). Divide evenly among the four ramekins. Top evenly with crushed Oreos.

Set the ramekins in a roasting pan. Pour hot, boiling water in the pan so that it comes halfway up the ramekins. Bake for 20-25 mins.

Remove the pan from the oven. Let the ramekins cool for 1 hour. Then cover with plastic & refrigerate until cold, at least 2 hours, and up to overnight.

About 10 mins before serving the Crème brulée, pull the custards out of the refrigerator.

To caramelize them under your broiler, preheat it and set the top rack in the upper two-thirds of the oven.

Sprinkle the remaining 8 tbsp sugar evenly over the top of the custards, using about 2 tbsp per ramekin.

If using a butane torch, carefully turn the flame directly onto the sugar. Broil or torch until the sugar turns brown, approximately 3 mins. Remove.

Let cool for before serving.

24) Orange Cherry Crème Brûlée

Delicious and tart Crème Brûlée recipe.

Makes: 4 servings

Prep: 30 mins

Cook: 25 mins

Ingredients:

- 2 cups heavy cream
- 5 egg yolks
- ½ tbsp. orange extract
- ½ tbsp. cherry extract
- 11 tbsp. sugar

Directions:

Preheat oven to 325°F.

In a saucepan over med-high heat, add the cream by heating it until it's almost simmering.

In the meantime, whisk the yolks + 3 tbsp of the sugar in a large bowl until the yolks get a bit thick.

Slowly whisk the cream into the yolk mixture. Stir in the orange and cherry extracts.

Pour mixture through a strainer into any container with a spout). Divide evenly among the four ramekins.

Set the ramekins in a roasting pan. Pour hot, boiling water in the pan so that it comes halfway up the ramekins. Bake for 20-25 mins.

Remove the pan from the oven. Let the ramekins cool for 1 hour. Then cover with plastic & refrigerate until cold, at least 2 hours, and up to overnight.

About 10 mins before serving the Crème brulée, pull the custards out of the refrigerator.

To caramelize them under your broiler, preheat it and set the top rack in the upper two-thirds of the oven.

Sprinkle the remaining 8 tbsp sugar evenly over the top of the custards, using about 2 tbsp per ramekin.

If using a butane torch, carefully turn the flame directly onto the sugar. Broil or torch until the sugar turns brown, approximately 3 mins. Remove.

Let cool for before serving.

25) Butterscotch Crème Brûlée

A classic Crème Brûlée recipe with notes of butterscotch extract

Makes: 4 servings

Prep: 30 mins

Cook: 25 mins

Ingredients:

- 2 cups heavy cream
- 5 egg yolks
- 1 tbsp. butterscotch extract
- 11 tbsp. sugar

Directions:

Preheat oven to 325°F.

In a saucepan over med-high heat, add the cream by heating it until it's almost simmering.

In the meantime, whisk the yolks + 3 tbsp of the sugar in a large bowl until the yolks get a bit thick.

Slowly whisk the cream into the yolk mixture. Stir in the butterscotch.

Pour mixture through a strainer into any container with a spout). Divide evenly among the four ramekins.

Set the ramekins in a roasting pan. Pour hot, boiling water in the pan so that it comes halfway up the ramekins. Bake for 20-25 mins.

Remove the pan from the oven. Let the ramekins cool for 1 hour. Then cover with plastic & refrigerate until cold, at least 2 hours, and up to overnight.

About 10 mins before serving the Crème brulée, pull the custards out of the refrigerator.

To caramelize them under your broiler, preheat it and set the top rack in the upper two-thirds of the oven.

Sprinkle the remaining 8 tbsp sugar evenly over the top of the custards, using about 2 tbsp per ramekin.

If using a butane torch, carefully turn the flame directly onto the sugar. Broil or torch until the sugar turns brown, approximately 3 mins. Remove.

Let cool for before serving.

26) Red Velvet Crème Brûlée

A hybrid of desserts! If you love red velvet, you're gonna love this recipe!

Makes: 4 servings

Prep: 30 mins

Cook: 25 mins

Ingredients:

- 2 cups heavy cream
- 5 egg yolks
- 2 tbsp. cocoa powder
- Red food colouring
- 1 tbsp. vanilla extract
- 11 tbsp. sugar

Directions:

Preheat oven to 325°F.

In a saucepan over med-high heat, add the cream by heating it until it's almost simmering.

In the meantime, whisk the yolks + 3 tbsp of the sugar in a large bowl until the yolks get a bit thick. Add in the cocoa powder, vanilla, and a little bit of red food coloring.

Slowly whisk the cream into the yolk mixture.

Pour mixture through a strainer into any container with a spout). Divide evenly among the four ramekins.

Set the ramekins in a roasting pan. Pour hot, boiling water in the pan so that it comes halfway up the ramekins. Bake for 20-25 mins.

Remove the pan from the oven. Let the ramekins cool for 1 hour. Then cover with plastic & refrigerate until cold, at least 2 hours, and up to overnight.

About 10 mins before serving the Crème brulée, pull the custards out of the refrigerator.

To caramelize them under your broiler, preheat it and set the top rack in the upper two-thirds of the oven.

Sprinkle the remaining 8 tbsp sugar evenly over the top of the custards, using about 2 tbsp per ramekin.

If using a butane torch, carefully turn the flame directly onto the sugar. Broil or torch until the sugar turns brown, approximately 3 mins. Remove.

Let cool for before serving.

27) Dark Chocolate Coffee Crème Brûlée

Dark chocolate Crème Brûlée with notes of coffee

Makes: 4 servings

Prep: 30 mins

Cook: 25 mins

Ingredients:

- 2 cups heavy cream
- 5 egg yolks
- ½ cup dark chocolate, chopped
- 1 tbsp. coffee
- 1 tbsp. vanilla extract
- 11 tbsp. sugar

Directions:

Preheat oven to 325°F.

In a saucepan over med-high heat, add the cream by heating it until it's almost simmering.

In the meantime, whisk the yolks + 3 tbsp of the sugar in a large bowl until the yolks get a bit thick.

Once the cream is done, add in the dark chocolate and coffee.

Then slowly whisk cream and chocolate mixture into the yolk mixture. Stir in the vanilla.

Pour mixture through a strainer into any container with a spout). Divide evenly among the four ramekins.

Set the ramekins in a roasting pan. Pour hot, boiling water in the pan so that it comes halfway up the ramekins. Bake for 20-25 mins.

Remove the pan from the oven. Let the ramekins cool for 1 hour. Then cover with plastic & refrigerate until cold, at least 2 hours, and up to overnight.

About 10 mins before serving the Crème brulée, pull the custards out of the refrigerator.

To caramelize them under your broiler, preheat it and set the top rack in the upper two-thirds of the oven.

Sprinkle the remaining 8 tbsp sugar evenly over the top of the custards, using about 2 tbsp per ramekin.

If using a butane torch, carefully turn the flame directly onto the sugar. Broil or torch until the sugar turns brown, approximately 3 mins. Remove.

Let cool for before serving.

28) Chocolate Coconut Crème Brûlée

Chocolate and coconut? Yes, please!

Makes: 4 servings

Prep: 30 mins

Cook: 25 mins

Ingredients:

- 2 cups coconut milk
- 5 egg yolks
- ½ cup bittersweet chocolate, chopped
- 1 tbsp. vanilla extract
- 11 tbsp. sugar

Directions:

Preheat oven to 325°F.

In a saucepan over med-high heat, add the coconut milk by heating it until it's almost simmering.

In the meantime, whisk the yolks + 3 tbsp of the sugar in a large bowl until the yolks get a bit thick.

Once the coconut milk is done, add in the chocolate.

Then slowly whisk coconut milk and chocolate mixture into the yolk mixture. Stir in the vanilla.

Pour mixture through a strainer into any container with a spout). Divide evenly among the four ramekins.

Set the ramekins in a roasting pan. Pour hot, boiling water in the pan so that it comes halfway up the ramekins. Bake for 20-25 mins.

Remove the pan from the oven. Let the ramekins cool for 1 hour. Then cover with plastic & refrigerate until cold, at least 2 hours, and up to overnight.

About 10 mins before serving the Crème brulée, pull the custards out of the refrigerator.

To caramelize them under your broiler, preheat it and set the top rack in the upper two-thirds of the oven.

Sprinkle the remaining 8 tbsp sugar evenly over the top of the custards, using about 2 tbsp per ramekin.

If using a butane torch, carefully turn the flame directly onto the sugar. Broil or torch until the sugar turns brown, approximately 3 mins. Remove.

Let cool for before serving.

29) Peanut Butter Crème Brûlée

Peanut butter lovers are going to love this simple yet delicious recipe.

Makes: 4 servings

Prep: 30 mins

Cook: 25 mins

Ingredients:

- 2 cups heavy cream
- 5 egg yolks
- ½ cup creamy peanut butter
- 11 tbsp. sugar

Directions:

Preheat oven to 325°F.

In a saucepan over med-high heat, add the cream by heating it until it's almost simmering.

In the meantime, whisk the yolks + 3 tbsp of the sugar in a large bowl until the yolks get a bit thick.

When the cream is done, add in the creamy peanut butter.

Then slowly whisk the cream mixture into the yolk mixture.

Pour mixture through a strainer into any container with a spout). Divide evenly among the four ramekins.

Set the ramekins in a roasting pan. Pour hot, boiling water in the pan so that it comes halfway up the ramekins. Bake for 20-25 mins.

Remove the pan from the oven. Let the ramekins cool for 1 hour. Then cover with plastic & refrigerate until cold, at least 2 hours, and up to overnight.

About 10 mins before serving the Crème brulée, pull the custards out of the refrigerator.

To caramelize them under your broiler, preheat it and set the top rack in the upper two-thirds of the oven.

Sprinkle the remaining 8 tbsp sugar evenly over the top of the custards, using about 2 tbsp per ramekin.

If using a butane torch, carefully turn the flame directly onto the sugar. Broil or torch until the sugar turns brown, approximately 3 mins. Remove.

Let cool for before serving.

30) White Chocolate Maple Crème Brûlée

White chocolate Crème Brûlée with maple syrup

Makes: 4 servings

Prep: 30 mins

Cook: 25 mins

Ingredients:

- 2 cups heavy cream
- 5 egg yolks
- ½ cup white chocolate, chopped
- 1 tbsp. maple syrup
- 11 tbsp. sugar

Directions:

Preheat oven to 325°F.

In a saucepan over med-high heat, add the cream by heating it until it's almost simmering.

In the meantime, whisk the yolks + 3 tbsp of the sugar in a large bowl until the yolks get a bit thick.

Once the cream is done, add in the white chocolate and maple syrup.

Then slowly whisk cream and chocolate mixture into the yolk mixture.

Pour mixture through a strainer into any container with a spout). Divide evenly among the four ramekins.

Set the ramekins in a roasting pan. Pour hot, boiling water in the pan so that it comes halfway up the ramekins. Bake for 20-25 mins.

Remove the pan from the oven. Let the ramekins cool for 1 hour. Then cover with plastic & refrigerate until cold, at least 2 hours, and up to overnight.

About 10 mins before serving the Crème brulée, pull the custards out of the refrigerator.

To caramelize them under your broiler, preheat it and set the top rack in the upper two-thirds of the oven.

Sprinkle the remaining 8 tbsp sugar evenly over the top of the custards, using about 2 tbsp per ramekin.

If using a butane torch, carefully turn the flame directly onto the sugar. Broil or torch until the sugar turns brown, approximately 3 mins. Remove.

Let cool for before serving.

Conclusion

There you have it! Delicious Crème Brûlée recipes for you to make! I hope you enjoyed this book and that you give each of these recipes a try. After all, you never know which one might end up being your favorite!

Biography

Food is like music, and Will knew that when he stepped into the restaurant business. Will loved food, and American classics were always a favorite. He loved the feelings and emotions some of this food invoked in him. Serving unique American dishes was one way to connect his love for music and food on a plate. Customers who would later come into his restaurant could instantly link classic American music stars to the food on their plates. This was a thought well appreciated by the diners.

Even more was that Will researched old and deep-rooted foods in American history, added his spin, and gave the customer a piece of history on the plate.

However, his career did not start in the food industry, but after working as a waiter in a couple of local and renowned All-American restaurants, he went back to culinary school to perfect his skills in plating dishes to aesthetically please the customers as they listened to music from back in the days.

Customers came to his restaurant not because he was a good cook, but to learn the American story behind the meals.

Today, Will has ventured into other food terrains, including serving original cocktails that pair incredibly well with steak and others. He has a restaurant and is making a difference in the lives of his customers.

Thank you

Did you like my book? I pondered it severely before releasing this book. Although the response has been overwhelming, it is always pleasing to see, read or hear a new comment. Thank you for reading this. And I would love to hear your honest opinion about it. Furthermore, many people are searching for a unique book, and your feedback will help me gather the right books for my reading audience.

Thanks!

Will C.

Made in the USA
Las Vegas, NV
15 December 2022

61960450R00057